MASTER YOUR MOTIVATION

A PRACTICAL GUIDE TO UNSTICK YOURSELF,
BUILD MOMENTUM AND SUSTAIN LONG-
TERM MOTIVATION (PERSONAL WORKBOOK)

THIBAUT MEURISSE

How to use this workbook

This workbook is to be used together with the book "Master Your Motivation: A Practical Guide to Unstick Yourself, Build Momentum and Sustain Long-Term Motivation (Personal Workbook)".

If you haven't grabbed "Master Your Motivation", you can get it at the URL below:

http://mybook.to/master_motivation

I encourage you to complete all the exercises in this workbook. The more effort you put into it, the better results you'll get and the better you'll feel about yourself.

Let's get started, shall we?

Stop —Do that one thing now!

Complete one task you've been putting off for a long time. And complete it now!

Ask yourself the following questions:

- What is the one task I know I should do but don't want to do?
- What one task, if I were to do right now, would free my mind the most?

PART I

ASSESS YOUR SITUATION

1. Accept your situation

Accept your current situation completely and show yourself compassion. Let go of any sense of guilt and remove the weight on your shoulder. It's time for a fresh beginning.

2. State the facts

Write down the raw facts regarding your current situation. Look at your situation objectively. What exactly happened?

What happened:

_____

_____

_____

_____

_____

_____

_____

_____

_____

_____

Then, ask yourself the following questions:

Will that even matter twenty years from now?

_____

Is it the first time I feel that way?

_____

Is it really that big of a deal?

_____

Is that event relevant on the world scale?

_____

What can I do about it now?

_____

_____

_____

_____

_____

_____

3. Find an external perspective

Seek an external perspective by doing one (or several) of the following:

a. Talk to a friend

Who could I talk to?

_____

When will I talk to that friend?

_____

b. See your situation from someone else's eyes

Who would that person be?

_____

What would they think?

_____

_____

_____

_____

_____

_____

c. Imagine your best friend being in a similar situation.

What would your best friend think?

_____

_____

_____

_____

_____

_____

What would you tell them? How would you support them?

_____

_____

_____

_____

_____

_____

PART II

BUILD MOMENTUM

1. Declutter

A. Reconnect with the present

Meditate on the fact that this moment is the only thing that will ever exist. The past is gone and the future has yet to come.

Write down any insight/thought below:

_____

_____

_____

_____

_____

_____

Transfer responsibility to your future you

Go through the three-step process below:

1. Take a few deep breaths and relax
2. Remember any past accomplishments and challenges you've overcome in the past. You've been able to survive up until now so your future self will do just fine. Imagine yourself transferring all your worries about your future to your future self. Feel yourself become lighter and more present (you can write down all your accomplishment using the win log at the end of this workbook).
3. Refocus on what you can do today and only on that.

Write down below what you can do today:

_____

_____

_____

_____

_____

_____

B. Sort out your worries

Fill in the table below:

What I worry about	Level of control (C/NC/SC)	How it benefits me	What I can do about it

C. Close open loops

Write down every task present in the back of your mind. Then, schedule time to complete these tasks.

Things to do:

-

-

-

-

-

-

-

-

-

-

-

-

-

-

-

-

-

D. Free up your schedule

Identify why you're not saying no

Fill in the table below:

Things I said yes to	Y/N (wanted to say yes or no?)	Why I couldn't say no

How to say no

a) Start small

What small favor(s) or invitation(s) could you say no to?

-

-

-

-

b) Stop over justifying yourself What will you say to decline the invitation(s)

Example:

- I'm sorry but parties are not my things so I'm going to skip this time.
- I'm sorry but right now I'm entirely focused on a very important project.

Write down below what you could say to decline invitation(s):

_____

_____

_____

_____

_____

_____

c) Practice saying no

Visualize a particular situation and see yourself saying no. What words would you use? How would you say them?

_____

_____

_____

_____

_____

_____

d) Offer alternatives

In the future, what alternative(s) could you offer instead of just saying yes or no? Write a few of them below:

-

-

-

-

-

Eliminate unpleasant tasks

Fill in the table below:

Your unpleasant tasks	What can you do about them (delegate them? Eliminate them? Reframe them?)

E. Declutter your desk

Remove anything necessary on your desk such as files you don't need right now, your smartphone etc.

F. Declutter your physical environment

Get rid of *everything* that you don't need to only keep things that bring your joy

1. Sort out your possession by categories (clothes, books, papers, miscellany and items with sentimental values)
2. Gather all the items in the first category, put the unnecessary ones in a plastic bag.
3. Move on to the next category and repeat the same process

G. Revise your forecast

When you set your daily goals, double the time you think you need to complete each of your tasks and see what happens.

H. Take breaks

Test one of the following techniques for a week:

1. Taking breaks every 75-90 minutes (with 10 to 15-minute breaks)
2. Taking breaks every 52 minutes (with 17-minute breaks)
3. Taking break every 25 minutes (with 5-minute breaks)

Which technique will you test in the next seven days?

_____

2. Focus

A. Assess your productivity

Create your time log using the time log table at the end of this workbook.

B. Leverage the 80/20 Principle

What are the 20% of your tasks that bring you 80% of your results?

For each of the areas below, write down the few things that if you were to do, would make a big difference.

Social life:

-

-

-

Finance

-

-

-

Health

-

-

-

Well-being

-

-

-

C. Destroy distraction

What one thing could you do right now to boost your motivation? If you feel any resistance, seek to identify the root of that resistance (fear of not being good enough, lack of clarity, lack of interest or lack of energy)

One thing I could do to boost my motivation is:

_____

_____

_____

_____

_____

_____

D. Optimize your environment

What could you change in your environment to feel more motivated and make it more likely you achieve your life goals?

What physical objects could add or remove?

_____

_____

_____

_____

Who could stop seeing or start hanging out with?

_____

_____

_____

_____

What changes could you make at home on at your workplace?

_____

_____

_____

_____

Other ways you will optimize your environment:

_____

_____

_____

_____

Digital detox

Experiment with full and partial detox:

Full detox: for 24 hours, 48 hours or more, refrain from using any digital device.

When will you start your full detox?

_____

Partial detox: create your own rules regarding your digital environment. For the next seven days, do your best to follow these rules you set and see how you feel.

When you will do with your seven-day partial detox?

_____

3. Reignite

A. Do more of what you love

Let go of what doesn't make you happy

Make a list of what you do every day. Then, ask yourself, "what are the activities that fail to bring me the sense of fulfillment I'm looking for?"

Activity	Level of fulfillment

Identify what you love to do

Answer the following questions:

When was the last time you had a great day and why? What did you do?

_____

_____

_____

_____

_____

_____

What are you looking forward to the most every day?

_____

_____

_____

_____

If you could do only one activity you love every day, what would that be?

_____

What activities, if you did, would allow you to feel good at the end of your day?

_____

_____

_____

_____

_____

How would you describe your ideal day to your best friend?

_____

_____

_____

_____

_____

Is there something you enjoyed doing in the past but stopped doing?

_____

Is there something you've always wanted to try but never muster the courage to?

_____

Write down 20 things you love to do:

1.

2.

3.

4.

5.

6.

7.

8.

9.

10.

11.

12.

13.

14.

15.

16.

17.

18.

19.

20.

B. Identify what really motivates you

Identify what you really want

Ask yourself the following questions:

Is it really my goal or is it someone else's goal?

_____

_____

_____

_____

Is it exciting me? Do I feel pulled by it or do I have to continuously push and struggle?

_____

_____

_____

_____

What will I gain from achieving that goal? And is it what I want? Will it really improve my life?

_____

_____

_____

_____

Find your strengths

Answer the following questions:

What are your biggest strengths?

_____

_____

_____

_____

What is it that you believe only you can do? What is unique about you?

_____

_____

_____

_____

What do you find so easy to do that you genuinely don't understand why others have difficulties doing it?

_____

_____

_____

_____

What people compliment you on? If you don't know, ask your friends, family members or colleagues

_____

_____

_____

_____

If you need help to find your strengths, check out my free ebook *Find What You Love* at the URL below:

https://whatispersonaldevelopment.org/find-what-you-love

Identify your core values

Fill in the table below:

	Top 5 core values	Living by then? (Y/N)	How could I better align with them?
#1			
#2			
#3			
#4			
#5			

Understanding your personality

Take the following test to help you better understand your personality.

Introversion test:

https://www.quietrev.com/the-introvert-test/

Briggs Myers's test (16 personalities):

http://www.humanmetrics.com/cgi-win/jtypes2.asp

Big Five Personality test:

https://www.truity.com/test/big-five-personality-test

Now, what one thing could you do to better express your personality?

Identifying your core values

Creating your vision

Write down your answer to the following questions:

a) How do you want the world to change as the result of your own actions?

_____

_____

_____

_____

b) What group of people, causes or organizations do you want to serve in this world?

_____

_____

_____

_____

c) If you could solve only one problem in the world, what would that be? Why?

_____

_____

_____

_____

d) What is your unique ways to express yourself to this world? What verbs best describe

_____

_____

_____

_____

C. Set exciting goals

a) Reconnecting with your original whys

Take some time to reconnect with your vision. Look at different areas one by one and ask yourself whether you're moving in the right direction. Observe the gap between where you are and what you aspire for.

Career:

Why did you choose your current career? What were your aspirations when you first got started? What motivated you?

_____

_____

_____

_____

_____

_____

Family:

What original vision did you have for you and your family? How could you close the gap between your csituation and what you aspire for?

_____

_____

_____

_____

_____

Relationship:

How did you feel at the beginning of your relationships? What were you deepest aspirations

_____

_____

_____

_____

_____

_____

Social life:

What the ideal social life for you? What could you do to move closer to this ideal?

_____

_____

_____

_____

_____

_____

b) Make new plans

Write down your answers to the following questions: what do I want?

Let your imagination go wild and make sure you pay attention to any sign of excitement you may experience.

Is there any goal or idea you feel drawn toward?

_____

_____

_____

_____

_____

_____

Is there anything that makes you feel really good?

_____

_____

_____

_____

_____

Is there something you feel like doing right now or can't wait to make happen in the near future?

_____

_____

_____

_____

_____

_____

Remember that how you feel is important. Your emotions tell you a lot about yourself and what you value the most.

c) Strengthening your why

Answer the question, "What's the most important (and exciting) goal I want to pursue right now?

Now, what are all the reasons it must happen?"

Come up with a list of at least twenty reasons you want to achieve that goal. If you can, try to come up with 100 reasons.

20 reasons it must happen:

1.

2.

3.

4.

5.

6.

7.

8.

9.

10.

11.

12.

13.

14.

15.

16.

17.

18.

19.

20.

4. Jump

A. Do the impossible

Write down everything you think you could never do. Now, select one thing in your list and commit to doing it this week or this month.

What I think I could never do

-

-

-

-

-

-

-

-

-

The one "impossible" thing I will do:

_____

B. Meet new people

Answer the following questions:

What type of people do I want to meet? And what are their values, vision, traits of character etc.)

_____

_____

_____

_____

_____

Where can I find them?

_____

_____

_____

_____

_____

_____

What concrete actions will I do to meet like-minded people?

_____

_____

_____

_____

_____

_____

C. Break old patterns

How do you think, feel and act now as opposed to before?

Remember a time you felt motivated. What were you thinking, feeling and doing? Spend a few minutes reconnecting with the way you felt.

	Before	Now
How I feel		
How I think		
How I act		

Do thing differently

What different activities could you engage in now? Write them down below:

-

-

-

-

-

D. Perform an act of kindness

Do one act of kindness today.

Your act of kindness:

---

5. Complete

A. Complete tasks one hundred percent

Write down below some unfinished projects.

-

-

-

-

How does that make you feel?

_____

_____

_____

_____

Now, remember a time you completed a project that was important to you.

How did you feel? And what happened after that? Did you feel more motivated? More confident? Write your answer below:

_____

_____

_____

_____

B. Destroy shiny object syndrome

Overcome distractions using the following steps:

- **Be aware:** See which area of your life you fall off track with your goals. Understand how success works and change your mindset accordingly.
- **Implement an effective strategy:** Spend time to craft an effective plan that, when you follow, will deliver the results you want. Don't reinvent the wheel. Instead, copy what people who've achieved your goal did.
- **Be patient:** Life is a marathon, not a sprint. Think long-term and you will do better than most people. Your mantras: "Be patient" and "it's okay you have time".
- **Be consistent:** Stay focus on a specific course of action and do that consistently every day until you achieve the results you want.
- **Overcome your fears:** be honest with yourself and face your fears instead of using procrastination as a way to stay within your comfort zone. Remember: action cures fear.
- **Commit:** Set a specific goal that excites you, establish a clear deadline and resolve to achieve that goal. Make it public or find an accountability partner or coach if needed.
- **Avoid information overload:** have a clear intent behind what you do, create a learning schedule and remove as many external stimuli as you possibly can. The more deliberate you are, the less overwhelmed you will feel.

C. Honor your promises

a) Keep your promises to others

What are some of the things you said to people you would do but haven't?

-

-

-

-

Do one of these things now.

The one thing you'll do:

_____

b) Keep your promises to yourself

For a week, set 3 simple daily tasks and complete them. Write down below the 3 daily tasks you'll complete for seven days:

1.

2.

3.

D. Procrastinate smartly

Write down all the small actions you could take right now. Try to lean towards activities you enjoy or at least, activities that move you in the right direction.

-

-

-

-

-

-

-

-

-

-

Now, select one action and resolve to take it now or, if you can't, later today.

Your one action:

_____

E. Deep dive

Identify one project you've started but haven't completed. Then, give yourself a short period of time to focus on it until it's complete one hundred percent.

One project you haven't completed:

_____

When you will complete it:

_____

PART III

SUSTAIN MOMENTUM

1. Acknowledge

A. Complete three tasks

Write down three tasks you want to complete today, finish them and celebrate your wins. Repeat the process every day until it becomes a habit.

Today's three tasks:

1.

2.

3.

B. Feel proud of yourself

Find something you're proud of and acknowledge yourself for that now. Say to yourself "I'm proud of you for *insert what makes you proud of yourself*."

I'm proud of myself for:

Then, before going to bed, think of three things you're proud of.

C. Right actions vs. right results

Look at goals you want to accomplish in various areas of your life. Identify the right actions for each of them. What are a few things that if you keep doing repeatedly would allow you to build momentum over time and eventually achieve your goals?

Goal #1

Right actions:

-

-

-

Goal #2

Right actions:

-

-

-

Goal #3

Right actions:

-

-

-

2. Commit

A. Seek external accountability

What is one thing you could do to build accountability? Write it down below:

_____

B. Create a morning ritual

Create your personalized morning ritual using the steps below:

1. **Clarifying your "why".** Write down your main objective below (feeling grateful, being more productive etc.)

_____

_____

_____

_____

2. **Getting excited.** Write down one or several activities you thoroughly enjoy and want to do first thing in the morning.

_____

_____

_____

_____

3. Identifying obstacles and preparing yourself mentally. Write down potential obstacles and visualize yourself dealing with them.

_____

_____

_____

_____

4. Selecting the components of your morning ritual. Select activities that will feed your body, mind and soul. Write them down below

_____

_____

_____

_____

5. Deciding how much time you have available. Write down how much time you will dedicate to your morning ritual

_____

_____

_____

_____

6. Removing roadblocks and distractions. Write down what you will do to remove frictions. (Prepare your running gears the day before etc.)

_____

_____

_____

_____

7. Setting yourself up for success. What will you do to make sure you get enough sleep so that you wake up energized and stick to your morning ritual?

_____

_____

_____

_____

8. Committing one hundred percent. Spend a moment to really commit to doing it.

9. Undertaking the 30-Day Challenge. Commit to sticking to your new morning ritual for 30 days. Write down below what morning ritual you commit to.

I commit to:

_____

C. Live with intent

Set daily intents using the step-by-step method below.

1. Write down the main segments of your day below (i.e, going to work, eating lunch etc.):

-

-

-

-

-

-

-

-

-

-

-

-

2. Select the segment(s) in which you want to feel different than you currently do.

-

-

3. Set a specific trigger for your intent. Write down your trigger below:

_____

4. Decide what you will do to change your emotional state. Create a sort of ritual before you enter that segment of your day. Write it down below:

_____

_____

_____

_____

5. Set reminders. If necessary, have something that reminds you of the intended action (post-it, timer etc.)

My reminder(s) are:

_____

_____

_____

_____

D. Commit to 30-day challenges

Implementing a 30-day challenge is a great way to build momentum and boost your motivation. Below is what you can do to make your 30-day challenge a success.

How to undertake a 30-Day Challenge successfully

Answer the following questions.

a) What would make the biggest impact on your life if you committed to start or stop doing it for thirty days?

_____

_____

_____

_____

b) What exactly do you commit to doing every day for the next thirty days?

_____

_____

_____

_____

c) *How will you create accountability for your challenge?* (who will be your accountability, how will you communicate and how often etc.

_____

_____

_____

_____

d) *What will happen if you fail?* (What are the consequences of not following through?)

_____

_____

_____

_____

e) *How will you reward yourself?*

_____

_____

_____

_____

E. Change your self-talk

Think of something you believe you can't do well. For instance, "I can't talk in front of an audience".

Then, replace the expression "I can't" with each of the expressions below.

- I can do/become...
- I will do/become...
- I want to do/become...
- I love doing/becoming...
- I choose to do/become...
- What if I could do/become...?
- Imagine if I could do/become...? How can I do/become...?
- What would I need to believe to be able to do/become...?
- How would it make me feel if I could do/become...?

Your turn now:

I can

I will

I want to

I love

_____

I choose to

_____

What if I could

_____

Imagine if I could

_____

How can I

_____

What would I need to believe to be able to

_____

How would I make me feel if I could

_____

F. Develop self-compassion

Undertake a 7-day compassion challenge. For the next seven days, wherever possible, refrain from criticizing yourself. To help you become aware of your negative self-talk, I encourage you to wear a rubber band around your wrist and to snap it whenever you notice any self-criticism. Then, give yourself words of encouragement. They could be something like:

- "I know you're struggling right now, but you're doing the best you can."
- "You're doing okay. Everybody goes through challenging times once in a while."
- "I'm proud of you. Even though you feel the urge to criticize yourself, you still make an effort to be kinder to yourself."

Don't get too caught up with the exact words you should use. Your intention to be gentle with yourself is what matters the most. Over time, you'll find the right words to encourage yourself and show yourself the compassion you deserve.

G. Practice daily gratitude

Practice one of the exercises below for at least 7 days:

a) Thank people

Sit down on a chair or lie down in your bed and close your eyes. Then, think of someone you know and thank him or her. It doesn't matter who the person is. Whenever possible, think of something specific they did for you. Perhaps, they gave you some advice, helped you learn an important lesson or brought you joy during the time you spent with them. Repeat the process.

b) Thank items in your life

Select one specific item in the room you're sitting in right now. For instance, it could be your desk or the chair you're sitting in. Then, take the time to appreciate it.

- Think of the way this item improves your life.
- Think of all the people involved in its creation.

c) Create a gratitude journal

Buy a journal and every time you receive a compliment, write it down in your journal.

d) Gratitude exercise

Every day when you wake, write down three new things you would like to acknowledge. Try to come up with three different things each morning.

e) Gratitude meditation

Listen to gratitude meditation and follow the instructions. You'll find many examples on YouTube.

The one gratitude exercise I will experiment with is:

PART IV

25 SIMPLE STRATEGIES TO GET YOUR MOTIVATION BACK

Motivation comes and goes but they are many things you can do to get your motivation back. Below are some techniques you can use to get out of a slump and start generating momentum:

A. Get it done

Use the completion principle to get your motivation back.

I. Complete a task you've been putting off for too long. Identify one task or project you've been putting off for a while and go complete it right now.

2. Write it down, get it done. Write down a list of all things you know you have to do but have been putting off. Now, schedule a block of time to complete them by batching them together.

3. Complete a simple and easy task. Work on a small task that moves you toward your goal. Then, if you feel like it, work on another one and see where it leads you.

4. Complete one specific project. Deep dive on a specific project you have left unfinished and complete it one hundred percent.

5. Complete three things today. Write down three simple tasks you want to complete today. Complete them, then cross them off your list and say to yourself "good job!". Reward yourself with your favorite treat or movie at the end of the day. Repeat this process tomorrow and the day after.

B. Give yourself a break

Take a step back and get out of your head. Things probably aren't as bad as you think.

6. Look at the facts. Take a step back and look at your current situation from a purely objective point of view. What are the facts?

Facts are no big deal but your interpretation can be. Will you remember your current situation twenty years from now? Is that really a big deal? If not, can you let go?

7. Talk to a friend. Call a friend or meet him or her to get a different perspective.

8. Hire a coach or find an accountability partner. Find someone you can work with. It will give you a new perspective and will create accountability making it more likely you take consistent actions.

9. Take a break. Perhaps, all you need is a break. Take your day off. Have a relaxing weekend and just do nothing.

10. Cultivate self-compassion. Give yourself a break. How you feel now is fine. Just let go of self-criticism and encourage yourself instead.

11. Do something for someone else. Helping other people prevent you from being overly focused on yourself and on your own problem. Who could you help today? Could you buy a gift for someone? Could you send a thank you letter? Could you help someone with his or her goals?

12. Exercise. Get your body moving. Go for a run. Work out. Do yoga. Exercise is a great way to get out of your mind and into your body.

C. Sort things out

Put some order in your life. Too much clutter can make you feel stuck.

13. Sort out your worries. Make a list of all the things you worry about. Next to each item write down whether you have control (C), some control (SC) or no control (C) over these things. Practice letting go of things you have no control over. For things you have (some) control over, write down what you can do about it.

14. Free up your schedule. Be ruthless with the way you use your time. Seek to remove any activities you don't enjoy or that don't move you toward your ideal vision.

15. Declutter your desk. A cluttered desk can be the manifestation of a cluttered mind. Clean your desk and your computer. Reorganize files on your computer.

16. Declutter your digital space. Clean up your email box, unsubscribe from newsletters, remove softwares you don't use etc.

17. Declutter your house. Spend your weekend decluttering your house. Only keep things you love and remove anything else. (See declutter your physical environment)

D. Get the excitement back

Focus on what you love and do right and get your motivation back.

18. De more of what you love. Schedule time during your day to do one of the things you love the most.

19. Ask yourself what excites you. Sit at your desk, take a pen and a piece of paper and write down "What do I love?". Then, write anything that comes to mind. See what projects, goals or ideas you feel drawn toward.

20. Start a new exciting challenge. Forget about your small goals. Think of a challenge that really excites you no matter how big or unrealistic it may seem. Then, take one action that move you forward whether it is buying a book, watching a video or contacting someone.

21. Celebrate your accomplishments. Take a piece of paper and write down everything you've ever accomplished in your life. Make sure you acknowledge yourself for personal problems you overcome. The more specific, the better.

22. Express gratitude. Cultivate the habits of expressing gratitude for all the things you have going on for you. Focus on the positive.

E. Reinvent yourself

Do something different. You can't do the same thing and expect different results.

23. Move beyond your comfort zone. Go do something a little bit scary. Do something you've never done before. Is there anything you've always wanted to try but never dare to? Go do that.

24. Meet new people. Who do you want to be surrounded with? Find a group of like-minded people and join it (use Meetup.com for instance). Or create your own group to attract people you want to meet.

25. Break old patterns. Spend your day doing things you don't normally do. Call an old friend, go for a walk etc.

Win Log

Write down below everything you've accomplished in your life. Aim at 50 things or more.

1.

2.

3.

4.

5.

6.

7.

8.

9.

10.

11.

12.

13.

14.

15.

16.

17.

18.

19.

20.

21.

22.

23.

24.

25.

26.

27.

28.

29.

30.

31.

32.

33.

34.

35.

36.

37.

38.

39.

40.

41.

42.

43.

44.

45.

46.

47.

48.

49.

50.

Time Log

Day 1	Day 2	Day 3	Day 4

Time Log

Day 5	Day 6	Day 7

NOTES:

Master Your Life With The Mastery Series

This book is the second book in the **"Mastery Series"**. You can check the other books at the following URL:

mybook.to/mastery_series

MASTER YOUR EMOTIONS (PREVIEW)

> " The mind in its own place, and in itself can make a
> heaven of Hell, a hell of Heaven.

— JOHN MILTON, POET.

We all experience a wild range of emotions throughout our lives. I had to admit, while writing this book, I experienced highs and lows myself. At first, I was filled with excitement and thrilled at the idea of providing people with a guide to help them understand their emotions. I imagined how readers' lives would improve as they learned to control their emotions. My motivation was high and I couldn't help but imagine how great the book would be.

Or so I thought.

After the initial excitement, the time came to sit down to write the actual book, and that's when the excitement wore off pretty quickly. Ideas that looked great in my mind suddenly felt dull. My writing seemed boring, and I felt as though I had nothing substantive or valuable to contribute.

Sitting at my desk and writing became more challenging each day. I started losing confidence. Who was I to write a book about emotions if I couldn't even master my own emotions? How ironic! I considered giving up. There are already plenty of books on the topic, so why add one more?

At the same time, I realized this book was a perfect opportunity to work on my own emotional issues. And who doesn't suffer from negative emotions from time to time? We all have highs and lows, don't we? The key is what we *do* with our lows. Are we using our emotions to grow? Are we learning something from them? Or are we beating ourselves up over them?

So, let's talk about *your* emotions now. Let me start by asking you this:

How do you feel right now?

Knowing how you feel is the first step toward taking control of your emotions. You may have spent so much time internalizing you've lost touch with your emotions. Perhaps you answered as follows: "I feel this book could be useful," or "I really feel I could learn something from this book." However, none of these answers reflect how you feel. You don't 'feel like this,' or 'feel like that,' you simply 'feel.' You don't 'feel like' this book could be useful, you 'think' this book could be useful, and that generates an emotion which makes you 'feel' excited about reading it. Feelings manifest as physical sensations in your body, not as an idea in your mind. Perhaps, the reason the word 'feel' is so often overused or misused is because we don't want to talk about our emotions. So, how do you feel now?

Why is it important to talk about emotions?

How you feel determines the quality of your life. Your emotions can make your life miserable or truly magical. That's why they are among the most important things to focus on. Your emotions color all your experiences. When you feel good, everything seems, feels, or tastes better. You also think better thoughts. Your energy levels are higher and possibilities seem limitless. Conversely, when you feel depressed, everything seems dull. You have little energy and you become unmotivated. You feel stuck in a place (mentally and physically) you don't want to be, and the future looks gloomy.

Your emotions can also act as a powerful guide. They can tell you something is wrong and allow you to make changes in your life. As such, they may be among the most powerful personal growth tools you have.

Sadly, neither your teachers nor your parents taught you how emotions work or how to control them. I find it ironic that just about anything comes with a how-to manual, while your mind doesn't. You've never received an instruction manual to teach you how your mind works and how to use it to better manage your emotions, have you? I haven't. In fact, until now, I doubt one even existed.

What you'll learn in this book

This book is the how-to manual your parents should have given you at birth. It's the instruction manual you should have received at school. In it, I'll share everything you need to know about emotions so you can overcome your fears and limitations and become the type of person you really want to be.

You'll learn what emotions are, how they are formed, and how you can use them for your personal growth. You'll also learn how to deal with negative emotions and condition your mind to create more positive emotions.

It is my sincere hope and expectation that, by the end of this book, you will have a clear understanding of what emotions are and will have all the tools you need to start taking control of them.

More specifically, this book will help you:

- Understand what emotions are and how they impact your life
- Identify negative emotions that control your life and learn to overcome them
- Change your story to take better control over your life and create a more compelling future, and
- Reprogram your mind to experience more positive emotions.

Here is a more detailed summary of what you'll learn in this book:

In **Part I**, we'll discuss what emotions are. You'll learn why you are wired to focus on negativity and what you can do to counter this effect. You'll also discover how your beliefs impinge upon your emotions. Finally, you'll learn how negative emotions work and why they are so tricky.

In **Part II**, we'll go over the things that directly impact your emotions. You'll understand the roles your body, your thoughts, your words, or your sleep, play in your life and how you can use them to change your emotions.

In **Part III**, you'll learn how emotions are formed. You'll also learn how to condition your mind to experience more positive emotions.

And finally, in **Part IV**, we'll discuss how to use your emotions as a tool for personal growth. You'll learn why you experience emotions such as fear or depression and how they work. You'll then discover how to use them to grow.

I. What emotions are

Have you ever wondered what emotions are and what purpose they serve?

In this section, we'll discuss how your survival mechanism affects your emotions. Then, we'll explain what the 'ego' is and how it impacts your emotions. Finally, we'll discover the mechanism behind emotions and learn why negative emotions can be so hard to deal with.

1. How your survival mechanism affects your emotions

Why people have a bias towards negativity

Your brain is designed for survival, which explains why you're able to read this book at this very moment. When you think about it, the probability of you being born was extremely low. For this miracle to happen, all the generations before you had to survive long enough to procreate. In their quest for survival and procreation, they must have faced death hundreds or perhaps thousands of times.

Fortunately, unlike your ancestors, you're (probably) not facing death every day. In fact, in many parts of the world, life has never been safer. Yet, your survival mechanism hasn't changed much. Your brain still scans your environment looking for potential threats.

In many ways, some parts of your brain have become obsolete. While you may not be seconds away from being eaten by a predator, your brain still gives significantly more weight to negative events than to positive ones.

Fear of rejection is one example of a bias toward negativity. In the past, being rejected from your tribe would reduce your chances of survival significantly. Therefore, you learned to look for any sign of rejection, and this became hardwired in your brain.

Nowadays, being rejected often carries little or no consequence to your long-term survival. You could be hated by the entire world and still have a job, a roof and plenty of food on the table, yet, your brain is still programmed to perceive rejection as a threat to your survival.

This is why rejection can be so painful. While you know most rejections are no big deal, you nevertheless feel the emotional pain. If you listen to your mind, you may even create a whole drama around it. You may believe you aren't worthy of love and dwell on a rejection for days or weeks. Worse still, you may become depressed as a result of this rejection.

In fact, one single criticism can often outweigh hundreds of positive ones. That's why, an author with fifty 5-star reviews, is likely to feel terrible when they receive a single 1-star review. While the author understands the 1-star review isn't a threat to her survival, her authorial brain doesn't. It likely interprets the negative review as a threat to her ego which triggers an emotional reaction.

The fear of rejection can also lead you to over-dramatize events. If your boss criticized you at work, your brain may see the event as a threat and you now think, "What if I'm fired? What if I can't find a job quickly enough and my wife leaves me? What about my kids?

What if I can't see them again?" While you are fortunate to have such an effective survival mechanism, it is also your responsibility to separate real threats from imaginary ones. If you don't, you'll experience unnecessary pain and worry that will negatively impact the quality of your life. To overcome this bias towards negativity, you must reprogram your mind. One of a human being's greatest powers is our ability to use our thoughts to shape our reality and interpret events in a more empowering way. This book will teach you how to do this.

Why your brain's job isn't to make you happy

Your brain's primary job is not to make you happy, but to ensure your survival. Thus, if you want to be happy, you must take control of your emotions rather than hoping you'll be happy because it's your natural state. In the following section, we'll discuss what happiness is and how it works.

How dopamine can mess with your happiness

Dopamine is a neurotransmitter which, among other functions, plays a major role in rewarding certain behaviors. When dopamine is released into specific areas of your brain—the pleasure centers—you get a high. This is what happens during exercise, when you gamble, have sex, or eat great food.

One of the roles of dopamine is to ensure you look for food so you don't die of starvation, and you search for a mate so you can reproduce. Without dopamine, our species would likely be extinct by now. It's a pretty good thing, right?

Well, yes and no. In today's world, this reward system is, in many cases, obsolete. While in the past, dopamine was linked to our survival instinct, The release of dopamine can now be generated artificially. A great example of this effect is social media, which uses psychology to suck as much time as possible out of your life. Have you noticed all these notifications that pop up constantly? They're used to trigger a release of dopamine so you stay connected, and the longer you stay connected, the more money the services make. Watching pornography or gambling also leads to a release of dopamine which can make these activities highly addictive.

Fortunately, we don't need to act each time our brain releases dopamine. For instance, we don't need to constantly check our Facebook newsfeeds just because it gives us a pleasurable shot of dopamine.

Today's society is selling a version of happiness that can make us *un*happy. We've become addicted to dopamine largely because of marketers who have found effective ways to exploit our brains. We receive multiple shots of dopamine throughout the day and we love it. But is that the same thing as happiness?

Worse than that, dopamine can create real addictions with severe consequences on our health. Research conducted at Tulane University showed that, when given permission to self-stimulate their pleasure center, participants did it an average of forty times per minute. They chose the stimulation of their pleasure center over food, even refusing to eat when hungry!

Korean, Lee Seung Seop is an extreme case of this syndrome. In 2005, Mr Seop died after playing a video game for fifty-eight hours straight with very little food or water, and no sleep. The subsequent investigation concluded the cause of death was heart failure induced by exhaustion and dehydration. He was only twenty-eight years old.

To take control of your emotions, it is essential you understand the role dopamine plays and how it affects your happiness. Are you addicted to your phone? Are you glued to your TV? Or maybe you spend too much time playing video games. Most of us are addicted to something. For some people it's obvious, but for others, it's more subtle. For instance, you could be addicted to thinking. To better control your emotions, it is important to shed the light on your addictions as they can rob you of your happiness.

The 'one day I will' myth

Do you believe that one day you will achieve your dream and finally be happy? This is unlikely to happen. You may (and I hope you will) achieve your dream, but you won't live 'happily ever after.' This is just another trick your mind plays on you.

Your mind quickly acclimates to new situations, which is probably the result of evolution and our need to adapt continually in order to survive and reproduce. This is also probably why the new car or house you want will only make you happy for a while. Once the initial excitement wears off, you'll move on to crave the next exciting thing. This phenomenon is known as 'hedonic adaptation.'

How hedonic adaptation works

Let me share an interesting study that will likely change the way you see happiness. This study, which was conducted on lottery winners and paraplegics, was extremely eye-opening for me. Conducted in 1978, the investigation evaluated how winning the lottery or becoming a paraplegic influence happiness:

The study found that one year after the event, both groups were just as happy as they were beforehand. Yes, just as happy (or unhappy). You can find more about it by watching Dan Gilbert's Ted Talk, The Surprising Science of Happiness.

Perhaps you believe that you'll be happy once you've 'made it.' But, as the above study on happiness shows, this is simply not true. No matter what happens to you, you'll revert back to your predetermined level of happiness once you've adapted to the new event. This is how your mind works.

Does that mean you can't be happier than you are right now? No. What it means is that, in the long run, external events have very little impact upon your level of happiness.

In fact, according to Sonja Lyubomirsky, author of *The How of Happiness*, fifty percent of our happiness is determined by genetics, forty percent by internal factors, and only ten percent by external factors. These external factors include such things as whether we're single or married, rich or poor, and similar social influences.

This suggests, only ten percent of your happiness is linked to external factors, which is probably way less than you thought. The bottom line is this: Your attitude towards life influences your happiness, not what happens to you.

By now, you understand how your survival mechanism impacts negatively your emotions and prevent you from experiencing more joy and happiness in your life. In the next segment/section we'll learn about the ego.

To read more visit my author page at:

amazon.com/author/thibautmeurisse

Made in the USA
Las Vegas, NV
06 September 2022

54803670R00055